T0122151

Book of Puzzle

Православие*

The One and Only Way for America to Succeed

ARTHUR NEWMARK

*Orthodoxy

ARCHWAY
PUBLISHING

Copyright © 2022 Arthur Newmark.

All rights reserved. No part of this book may be used or reproduced by
any means, graphic, electronic, or mechanical, including photocopying,
recording, taping or by any information storage retrieval system
without the written permission of the author except in the case of
brief quotations embodied in critical articles and reviews.

This book is a work of non-fiction. Unless otherwise noted, the author
and the publisher make no explicit guarantees as to the accuracy of
the information contained in this book and in some cases, names of
people and places have been altered to protect their privacy.

Archway Publishing books may be ordered through booksellers or by contacting:

Archway Publishing
1663 Liberty Drive
Bloomington, IN 47403
www.archwaypublishing.com
844-669-3957

Because of the dynamic nature of the Internet, any web addresses or
links contained in this book may have changed since publication and
may no longer be valid. The views expressed in this work are solely those
of the author and do not necessarily reflect the views of the publisher,
and the publisher hereby disclaims any responsibility for them.

ISBN: 978-1-6657-1709-0 (sc)
ISBN: 978-1-6657-1708-3 (hc)
ISBN: 978-1-6657-1710-6 (e)

Print information available on the last page.

Archway Publishing rev. date: 01/21/2022

Don't try to get it with your mind,
Don't try to fit in your dimention:
There is no Russia of your kind—
Here your belief is only mention.

Fyodor Tyutchev
November 28, 1866

PREFACE

Dear reader,

We do not know each other. I do not even know what language you speak. But I know for sure that this book will suit you. You have a book in your hands that you do not have to read. However, you will have to work hard on the mystery that I have hidden for you in its title. Yes, you still read a lot, but you have stopped pondering the true content of this or that novel, story, or verse. You want easiness without comprehension. Since you are holding this book in your hands, it means that you have already started thinking.

Each of us has our own idea of success. This story is about why Православие, in my opinion, is the only way for America to succeed. This story is the work of twenty years of scientific research that I have conducted in Russia, the United States, the Vatican, Israel, and Armenia. It is very important for me to suggest it to you—my American reader. I will explain why. It is here in the US that I have gotten acquainted with American society, which I associate with the story of Noah's ark, where representatives of all countries of the world live under the same laws and under one nation. This is wonderful. America itself seems to me as Noah's ark, moving towards global success.

You are holding in your hands an invitation. If you are used to reading comfortably on the couch, then get up, because you are going to a magical land, a land of fairy tales. You are going to Russia.

You might think that I will begin to acquaint you with the country, its laws and customs, cities and people, and its nature. Or you might think that I will introduce you to art and works, history or religion. Such is not the case. Everything is much more complex. I will introduce you to the Russian spirit … and the scent of Old Russia! All you need to do is to erase all your knowledge about Russia and start from scratch—from the same blank slate as the pages in my book.

Well, now I am leaving you alone with yourself. To help you, I have given you hints. I hope they will lead you to the key to true success.

Turn the page and you arrive.

CONTENTS

Hard to be a God.

Arkady and Boris Strugatsky
1964

Printed in the United States
by Baker & Taylor Publisher Services